The Absence of Light

Christie Hardwick

Tehom Center Publishing is a 501(c)3 nonprofit publishing feminist and queer authors, with a commitment to elevate BIPOC writers.

Paperback ISBN: 978-1-966655-74-9

Ebook ISBN: 978-1-966655-75-6

Contents

*I dedicate this book to our children's spouses
and our amazing grandchildren — Jason, Gita, and Jacque,
who gave us Burton, Harrison, Emma, Penny, Tessa, Charlotte, and Jack.*

Acknowledgments

In writing this book, I acknowledge those who don't need to read it: those rising to the occasion, speaking truth to power, giving their best to this moment, or building on the foundations they created. I'll mention a few by name, who also happen to be my friends: Kevin Jennings, Robert Banks, Kristen Kendricks, Melissa Sawyer, Nadine Smith,Toni Armstrong Jr., Rea Carey, Selisse Berry, Celine Oskuwu, Rayona Sharpnack, Kathy Levinson, Naomi Fine,Dr. LaDonna Butler, Terri Lipsey Scott, Jane Bunker, Temple Hayes, Simran Singh, Brian McNaught, and Rev. Kate Wilkinson.

Foreword

Christie Hardwick delivers a blunt self-reckoning: comfort, privilege, and spiritual bypassing kept her from acting with the urgency the moment demanded. The book is a public inventory of her own complicity in the social, political, and moral crises threatening democracy. But it is also a framework for self-forgiveness, renewed engagement, and building beloved community. The central premise: love in action requires radical accountability, not just good intentions

What stands out in these pages is not whether every assessment Christie makes will resonate with every reader. That is beside the point. The power of this book comes from watching someone do the kind of disciplined self-examination most of us avoid. It is like watching an athlete strengthen underused muscles. She stretches at angles that are uncomfortable. She asks questions most people deflect. She refuses to cushion her own choices with soft rationalizations. Even if you disagree with some parts of her accounting, the rigor of the process is undeniable and instructive.

Christie shows how easily we confuse the sense of being right with actually being informed. She examines how comfort can masquerade as wisdom, how spiritual language can soften truths that need to stay sharp, and how quickly curiosity can fade when our stories about ourselves go untested. She identifies the habits that quietly narrow our world and admits how those habits showed up in her own life.

She insists that a functioning democracy depends on people who are willing to update their beliefs, examine their defaults, and stay proximate to the people and problems they claim to care about, close enough that the consequences are no longer theoretical. That is the antidote to the rigidity that has taken root across public life. It is also the antidote to the unteachability that destabilizes institutions when people decide that certainty is more comfortable than truth.

What gives this book its weight is that Christie does not present herself as flawless or finished. She moves through remorse, forgiveness, and renewed engagement with a steady hand. She treats accountability as recalibration rather than punishment. She shows how a person can take a hard look at their choices without collapsing into shame or rushing to soften the picture.

The way forward she offers is practical: begin again, stay curious, stay connected, choose engagement over distance, and build beloved community as a daily habit rather than an abstract ideal. You don't need to mirror her conclusions to benefit from the clarity of her process. The real gift of this book is the demonstration of a mind and heart willing to do the work rather than perform the comfortable and familiar.

Christie reminds us that redemption is not an event. It is a choice made over and over. To stay awake. To adjust course. To treat love as something that must be carried into public life, not just held in private.

That is the invitation of this book.

And it is worth accepting.

Nadine Smith
Co-founder Equality Florida
CEO Color of Change

It is said that peace is more than the absence of war.
Perhaps darkness is more than the absence of light.

Introduction

I expected to be writing my third book in a trilogy.

The first book, *Radical Self-Tenderness*, was about how nurturing our own souls can help heal the world. It was about the importance and the possibility of each of us becoming what I call "tenderness broadcasting stations." It was about being a force for good in the world by including being good to yourself. I spent a year doing workshops in person and online, helping people wrap their heads and hearts around the idea of tenderness toward themselves. Some needed to define tenderness because it wasn't even a concept they considered, and others were tender toward everyone except themselves and had to explore, as I did, why.

I have heard from many that the practice of radical self-tenderness changed their relationship with themselves and spilled over into all their relationships. They experience more vulnerability and intimacy, and of this I am glad.

The second book, To *What End?*, *An Inquiry*, grapples with the question of what our great aim in life is. I wandered through the phases of my life, noting how the intentions, goals, achievements changed along the way. I recalled after my fifth decade how all the accumulation and desires for more faded into a new desire for greater connection and impact.

I asked, "What now?" I landed on love—to love both deep and wide, and to get better and better at it. Loving deep focused on the people closest to us in our constellation. How deeply can I love my partner, my children, my friends? And then I looked at whether it mattered how many people we included in our love or if loving our own constellation constituted a fulfilled life.

I came to realize that loving wide is a way of being: acting as love in all your encounters to the best of your ability each time.

So the second book considers love both deep and wide. It considers that aspirations for success, material wealth, the ideal life constantly change as we grow in our understanding of life and why we are here.

I came to know that there is no greater aspiration than to love well, and use love as the foundation for all we do. Love makes for a more peaceful, just world. And a peaceful, just world has to start within each one of us.

Love In Action

I continue to ask myself the question, "To what end?" And I unequivocally answer, "To be love in action."

To that end, this book is a confession and a blueprint for hope. I am accountable but not irredeemable. There are many social science views that would examine why I have acted or not acted in the ways I have. This book is not about the social science behind what motivates our behavior—although it is a fascinating study. This book is about one human taking inventory of how she contributed to the current paradigm of greed and othering that plagues us now.

One of the ways I share my love is by writing. I write to get clear and to stimulate my own and others' imaginations about fully living our lives. My intention was to write the third book now. I tentatively called it Is *It OK to Be Happy in a World Full of Suffering?* I expected to answer affirmatively and emphatically yes. Not only is it OK, but it is necessary as my outline suggests.

Instead, interrupted by the flurry of destructive actions coming from the U.S. White House, I felt prompted to write about my role in the dismantling of our democracy and, in effect, the world order. I believe each of us matters to the whole. Specifically, my philosophy is that we are all made of the same stuff. We share a planet. What each of us thinks, says, and does matters to the whole.

So I'll take you on my journey, where initially there is an absence of light but where eventually we find redemption in an engaged way of living, one that brings beloved community into the promise of a new day.

This book isn't written to make anyone feel bad, although it likely will. I wrote this book to face the truth of our own complicity with a world we don't want to inhabit. This book required me to move out of my own echo chamber and out of the comfort of having others always agree with and amplify my thoughts. This book establishes a new now, one in which I cannot claim ignorance or impediment, but one where I must claim awareness and choice.

First, the confessions, then the impact, then the remorse, then the way forward.

Who Am I to Write This?

I grew up in Silicon Valley when it was still orchards and open fields. I lived in neighborhoods where it was OK to trick or treat miles from your home, using a pillowcase to hold the bounty. I went to local schools that were primarily white and where I was one of three Black students all through high school. I attended a local Jesuit university on scholarship and graduated with honors.

During my college years, I married and had twin children. My husband and I divorced by the time I graduated. I went to work in the technology sector because I was a single mom of two kids and couldn't afford to be the teacher I planned to be. I moved up in my career because I was gifted with good looks and an active intelligence.

I met my second husband when I was twenty-six. We had a son together, and our marriage lasted eight years. I took off time from my high tech career to create a business with a dear friend and colleague for a few years. I went back to a corporate job once my youngest started school. I was elected to my local school board for two terms and eventually became an executive in a billion-dollar company.

Through every type of therapy under the sun—breathwork, talk, workshops, fire walking, pole climbing, wilderness retreats—I found my way to myself. All my therapeutic searching led me to leave corporate life. I went to school for four years, while building a coaching business, to become a licensed minister with Centers for Spiritual Living. I practiced my ministry as an executive coach and mentored with a spiritual lens. Eight years of practice earned my ordination, which has allowed me to marry more than one-hundred couples and provide guidance to hundreds of leaders.

My third marriage was to a woman when I was forty-six. We've had an amazing twenty years of traveling the world, enjoying life and our seven grandchildren between us.

These are the milestones of my life, but they do not cover my emotional journey, my spiritual search, my physical trauma, or any of the daily vestiges of life that shaped me. This is a glimpse at who wrote this book, these words. They came rushing through me, and I got out of the way.

This book is the result.

With all sincerity I also say, this book has nothing to do with people who live their purpose to the best of their ability and feel they give to their calling what they have to give. I say to you, keep doing what you are doing, and write me a note so I can celebrate you and learn from you. I'll even go so far as to say there are people I know who should not read this book. They are examples of how to live full out and give the best of themselves to the world.

This is for those of us who are falling short, and we know it.

1

First, the Confessions

THIS CHAPTER IS SIMPLY the list of transgressions as I see them. As you read them, you may feel some resistance, some defensiveness arise. If that happens, just notice it and keep reading.

Following is my list of transgressions. Is there something else you would have listed? Are there some that you are sure shouldn't be included? Make a note and see if the following chapters, which go into more depth in explaining these confessions, change anything in your thinking.

And for those who find themselves triggered by the term "confessions," think about it as reflections or discernments. I am taking inventory in a way that works for me, and I imagine there will be others who find it relevant.

My List

- I didn't care enough. I knew about conditions that were harmful or unfair. I felt compassion, and then I turned away.
- I didn't learn enough. I didn't understand both the local and the geopolitical landscape so I could act responsibly. You can't take informed action without being informed.
- I didn't act enough. I voted. I made some calls. But I didn't act with urgency or visibility or consistency.

Christie Hardwick

I didn't care enough because:

- I cared about my own constellation.
- I cared about my personal well-being.
- I cared about my pleasure and my bucket list.
- I cared about keeping peace and avoiding confrontation.
- I cared about many causes—the climate, refugees, LGBTQ+, Black Lives Matter, youth empowerment, homelessness, child trafficking, nature conservation, reproductive freedom, and the list goes on. But I became a checkbook philanthropist.
- I cared enough to write a check but not enough to understand the cause.

I didn't learn enough or do enough because:

- I didn't want to face conflict.
- I wanted to enjoy life.
- I supported other activists doing the work.
- I didn't want to believe the conspiracy theorists.
- I was comfortable.
- I had tools to get out of any discomfort.
- I had spiritual ideas to shield me.
- I leaned on spiritual practices to transcend pain.
- I relied on love and an open heart as solution.
- Like John Lennon, I hoped that "they" would join me.
- My corporate training let me compartmentalize.
- My elitism was fed and nurtured by my choices.
- I liked feeling exceptional.

I said I believed in the beloved community but I forgot:
The beloved community doesn't arise without effort.
The beloved community requires care, maintenance, and engagement.

2

Did I Care Enough?

- I didn't care enough. I knew about conditions that were harmful or unfair. I felt compassion, and then I turned away.
- I cared about my own constellation.
- I cared about my personal well-being, my pleasure, and my bucket list.
- I cared about keeping the peace and avoiding confrontation.
- My corporate training taught me to compartmentalize
- My choices fed and nurtured my elitism.
- I liked feeling exceptional.

I TREATED caring as if it were a finite substance. If there were only so much to go around, then I needed to focus. First I focused on work and having enough money to care for my children. Then I focused on staying sane and healthy enough to care for my children. Once I had some breathing room, I cared about experiencing some pleasure. I started to do a little traveling, consumed great food and a lot of alcohol.

I also gave myself the gift of volunteering. I said yes to serving on a board of a nonprofit dealing with death and dying, a position I held for a decade. I received as much from them as I gave.

I cared about my neighbor who was several decades my senior and who loved me and my children like her own.

This was my world for my first four decades of my life. I cared about my immediate constellation: children, friends, colleagues. I added more causes to care for as I got older, but I admit to not caring enough about people and things outside my immediate experience.

In my fifth decade, I had the opportunity to work with stellar leaders and to influence organizations to treat their employees with more dignity and respect. I didn't make sure the employees actually saw the benefits of the plans we created, nor did I call out the leadership when I knew they were not being fair or just.

During that time, for five years I had the privilege of being a member of The Women's Leadership Board for the Kennedy School of Government at Harvard. I did not attend Harvard, but I had the opportunity to influence powerful women who held the reins of wealth and large corporate interests. I was the co-chair of strategic planning for the group. My company sponsored me, and when I left the company, women on the board stepped up to sponsor me. I left the board because it wasn't convenient for me to spend the resources necessary to be there. I didn't think of the privilege, opportunity, or service I was bringing to many people I would never know.

I clearly remember once speaking at the front of a large assembly room, hundreds of women in attendance, and many standing at the back. I was speaking about our strategy to keep women at the forefront of policy at the university and beyond. The then-president of the Tom Peters Company was my co-presenter. After the presentation, several Black women students at the Kennedy School came to tell me how meaningful it was, how important it was, to see me (who looked like them) take charge of the room in the way I had.

I didn't care enough to stay, even after repeated attempts to sponsor, support, and subsidize my participation.

The Women's Leadership Board was just one example of opportunities to care, to see the bigger picture, to include others in my consideration. Other examples include the decision not to run for higher office in my state and to leave corporate leadership when I still had the opportunity to influence working conditions for thousands of people.

Caring Just Enough

I have a thousand excuses about why I didn't care enough: There's too much to care about. I can't care about everything. I can't fix everything, so why put too much caring into it? I didn't create it. I can only care so much. I can care for what's in front of me, I have limited resources and time. It's OK to be eighty/twenty, spending eighty percent of my energy on my personal needs and twenty percent caring for others. Who else will care for me?

And the rationalizations went on and on.

The impact of caring just enough looks like this. I care about the environment, the climate crisis, the destruction of the coral reefs, the destruction of the rainforest. These things cause pain in my heart when I think about them. And that's the rub. I limit how much I think about them. I limit my involvement to an occasional article, discussion, or support of a non-government organization (NGO) working on these issues. And meanwhile, I continue to fly in planes many times a year, not to work but to enjoy places and people that fill me with joy. I contribute to the carbon footprint that contributes to the changes in climate, the changes in climate that contribute to the devastating impact on nature.

The changes in climate don't personally affect me in any direct way, but I am aware of the people who have food and water scarcity because of overly warm weather in their region. I can't name them or their country without an internet search because they are not personal to me. They are a picture of people carrying buckets to find water and children eating monochromatic slop that's provided by an intervening NGO.

Finding a Path to True Caring

As an example of what caring looks like, we have friends, Dorothy and Tina, who care about the environment. They founded an art installation where we lived on Cape Cod that invited artists to use recycled materials and create art pieces in a small forest area that could be viewed as you walk and experience nature, and then you receive a message about how to better care for the Earth. These brilliant people also bought some land and now live sustainably, off the grid, farming, capturing sun energy, and living off the land. They cared enough to live differently.

In my own life, I have trouble sticking to a diet. I vacillate between eating only whole plant-based food and adding fish, even as I know there is over-fishing and that my selecting it on a menu contributes to that issue. I tell myself I'm supporting the livelihood of fishermen and women who rely on our consumption to live comfortable lives. Yet I know this is not sustainable in many places. Which places is it OK to eat fish? It's too much to keep track of. I try to keep track of the list of foods and supplements that are supposed to keep my body running optimally, and I don't even do that well. If I cared enough, wouldn't that look like a clear program for eating?

The twenty-plus years I spent in corporate America shaped some of my attitudes. My final years there as a highly paid executive taught me the skill of compartmentalization. I could do my job and get my bonuses without considering whether my company was a beneficial presence on the planet or not. I didn't take time to know.

I can make the excuse that I went to high tech for the money to take care of my children, and my prior idea to be a teacher was financially less attractive. I can say I was surviving through depression and was therefore unaware of the larger picture. I can say I knew my calling was not to work in technology but to be a creative, but I believed I couldn't afford that either.

I didn't care enough to figure out what, as Howard Thurman says, would "make me come alive."

Even if I feel pain and sadness about child trafficking, about violence against women all over the world, I kept ordering from Amazon and finding the best deal on business-class tickets so I could skip the line.

Sure, I earned the money. But once the figures got bigger and bigger, I stopped asking why I could earn so much to manage a manufacturing environment and earn so little if I were a teacher? Occasionally I'd feel a deep sense of depression over my privileges, like when I could afford to keep my teenage son safe by putting him in residential therapy. I contemplated for days how unfair it was that another mother wouldn't have this opportunity. But I didn't start a nonprofit to solve for it. I realized my son, like many young men, needed a set of rituals, of meaningful engagement to develop as men, but I didn't create anything to answer to it. I just took care of my own.

In many ways, because of my resources, while not in the top one percent of wealth, I enjoy elite experiences. I go on riverboat cruises, live part time in Italy, and participate in timeshares in wonderful locales. I didn't question why I should continue to do these things. I didn't question what impact they had on others. And I didn't often question if I should use my resources in a different way. I liked having exceptional adventures: seeing elephants in the wild, taking a boat with twelve friends around the Galapagos Islands, being with twenty-six people on a sailing yacht on the Dalmation Coast, bringing my children and grandchildren to luxury resorts.

Even as I enjoyed an amazing life, I cared about a lot of things happening in the world that caused suffering. Yet, based on my actions, I cared most about getting the most out of life. The things that caused pain in my heart, I soothed with taking some action like signing a petition or writing a check to an organization or supporting a leader who was doing something about it.

Watching What It Means to Care Deeply

I had earlier wonderful examples of caring in my life that could have led to different behavior from me. When I was nineteen years old, I arrived hot and very pregnant to look at an apartment with my then husband. The woman who lived next door to the apartment building made her way over to us and offered me a glass of water because she could see how I was suffering in the heat with my big belly and swollen ankles.

That glass of water became a lifeline all the years we lived there. When my twins were born, she came to help me set them up on cushions so I could breastfeed. She baked cookies for us every week and watched the babies while I went down the stairs to the laundry. I was in a stupor, getting very little sleep, and totally unprepared to manage a household.

My neighbor's name was Helen. She cared for us through the end of that first marriage to my next marriage and next child. We went to visit her one day at her home in Pacific Grove, California, when she was in her eighties. She gave me back every card I had written to her, carefully placed in an album. I realized she must be dying, and she allowed me to be with her the day before she left the planet. She thanked me for being in her life.

She cared so much for us that it helped me make it through many challenges. We weren't her family. She had a son, granddaughters, and a husband. Yet she extended herself to make us a part of her closest constellation. We were included in her heart and in her actions, every day. Helen helped me see myself as worthy because she offered her help at every turn. She encouraged me and never judged my inadequate parenting. Her warm embrace and her hot chocolate chip cookies, fresh out of the oven, were a balm to a nineteen-year-old mom.

The apartment we rented next to Helen's home may not have happened at all if I hadn't been attending the university just a few blocks away. In March of my senior year in high school, my guidance counselor, Ms. Cunningham, asked, "Hey Hardwick, where you going to school in September?" She presumed I had a plan, but I hadn't even considered it. My parents had not gone to college and only one of my siblings who left home early had. My mother thought I should just get a job and think about finding a suitable marriage within her church.

Ms. Cunningham had other ideas. She called me into her office and reminded me that I was graduating top of my class and that I would be eligible for a scholarship. She helped me apply, get an essay done, provided a recommendation, and, by the end of the school year, I had a full ride to a local private Jesuit university.

She cared enough to act, to see it through, and my life took a different direction because of her caring.

The commitment and follow-through that Helen and Ms. Cunningham demonstrated was caring enough. I did not emulate them. I stuck to my constellation, helping my sister out of trouble a few times, completely unaware of anyone outside my constellation whom I might care about. I didn't care enough, and that leads us to the next chapter and the next failing. I hadn't learned enough. When you learn about things, you deepen your care about them. And when your care is deep enough, you take action to protect them.

3

Identifying and Challenging
Our Comfort Zones

- *I didn't learn enough to understand that to delve into the local and geopolitical landscape is to act responsibly. You can't take informed action without being informed.*
- *I didn't want to face conflict.*
- *I didn't want to believe the conspiracy theorists.*
- *I was comfortable.*

I READ a lot and always have. I love to learn and always have. I gather information and make connections and think of myself as having a grasp of how the world works. It is my understanding that if what you learn doesn't change your approach or how you navigate the world, the learning was superficial.

I read Angela Davis. Decades ago she laid out how Palestine and other struggles of Black and Brown people across the globe connected to the struggles of Black people in my own country. I read about the connection of mass incarceration and the previous times of Jim Crow and slavery. I heard her, but I kept working at my job, accumulating my stuff, buying bigger homes and occasionally feeling bad about it.

I read about human trafficking, and I was appalled, horrified, sad, disgusted. And I didn't learn how it worked, who was behind it, why it perpetuated. So in denial of facts, I ended up living in a place (Florida) for several years, which turned out to be one of the most prolific hubs of human trafficking in the country. Right where I lived, women and children (primarily) were being enslaved, abused, and violated. And I rode my bike to the beach and enjoyed the views.

I remember learning that most of the laws our U.S. Congress passed were opposed to what the majority of their constituents demanded. There were available statistics that bore out the gross negligence of much of our representation. Nevertheless, I did not dive deeper to see how long this has been happening and to see if there were any differences in the two party system we had.

I had heard from more informed people that our federal legislators of both parties were all bought off by corporations, but I didn't learn more. As a matter of fact, when Citizens United was proposed, I remember having a literal wake up call. I woke up in the night and had the thought, "This is really wrong. This will cause so many problems in our elections and legislative bodies. Corporations are not people!" The next day, I called and emailed nonprofit leaders and people I thought were closer to the action. To a person, they didn't share my alarm, so I let it drop. I didn't learn more about it. I didn't continue communicating my concerns. Citizens United slipped into our electoral process without much of a peep. And today we know how much money corporations contribute to politics and how much they control the political and cultural narrative and outcomes.

The Politics of Wealth

I recently heard journalist Joy Reid lay out the history of wealth, poverty, and taxes in the United States. She argued that there were and are very, very wealthy people who never believed there should be an income tax. She reminded her audience that income taxes only became law in 1913.

She articulated that there are powerful wealthy people who oppose anti-poverty programs, many believing that all poverty is a function of effort and not opportunity. There are people who believe a class system or caste system is natural and should be allowed to flourish.

If I had paid more attention, would I have seen these ideas unfolding as public policy in the United States? If powerful wealthy people, those who have more resources than more than ninety percent of the people, don't want taxation that pays for social programs, that can lift people out of poverty, doesn't it make sense that we would continue to suffer the impacts of poverty, especially since big money can give unlimited sums to pay politicians to do their bidding?

I knew in the back of my mind that this was happening. I knew that corporate interests funded most elected representatives. I knew this because I knew of the few who were not. I knew of those few who would not accept corporate money because they knew that it came with powerful expectations.

I knew this, but I didn't act as if I did. I didn't make it central to my decisions and votes. I might as well have not learned it.

The Nature of U.S. Foreign Policy

When I read about world events or heard them on a news channel, I accepted most of what I learned at face value. China bad; Russia bad; U.S. good; Europe good. I accepted it all, even though in the 1990s, I went on a political study visit to Egypt and Israel. I saw with my own eyes and heard with my own ears about the self-serving nature of U.S. foreign policy. It was the first time I saw our country's footprint and understood that it wasn't altruistic.

When I took that trip, I was in my early thirties. Up to that time, I had a naive view that the U.S. was all about making everyone free and safe. I didn't take the time to learn about how capitalism really works. I never studied the ideas that demonstrate how democracy and capitalism are not truly compatible.

I had to look up the definition of capitalism to realize I had presumed we were a capitalist society because I witnessed so much greed. Because I didn't understand that regulating business kept us from truly being capitalist and dropping all social safety nets, I didn't truly respect or protect what we do have. I knew there needed to be regulations on business because greed could and had exploited people, the planet, and our natural resources, but I took these regulations for granted and didn't know there was work afoot to remove them.

I lived in a state and national system and I did not fully understand how it actually functioned.

Act Locally to Understand Globally

I got close to a local understanding of how our country works by becoming a member of my local school board. I was a trustee who oversaw a $120 million budget for education.

I got proximate with the system of governance at the local level. I was elected twice to represent my 30,000-student school district in the town where we lived in the 1990s. I took the same oath of office to uphold the U.S. Constitution as all elected people do.

I saw how hard it was to stay in integrity and on track for the students and teachers, and unions with all the pressure from the parents, the state, and the federal government. I gave it two terms, eight years of my life, while I worked a full-time job.

After my two terms on the school board, I spent more years dedicated to the idea of improving our education system by joining a nonprofit board as the founding chair of GreatSchools.org. I also joined the board of directors of GLSEN—the Gay, Lesbian, Straight, Education Network—that worked to end bullying of LGBTQ+ students.

I am not surprised by the state of our education system, I saw its flaws up close. As a result of my time in governance in a school system and in two NGOs, I had expertise, but I left it behind to continue to pursue success in the private sector. Whatever I learned eventually stopped driving my behavior. Even though I had learned enough, the issue of caring enough came back into play.

I was asked to run for the next level of political office, the state assembly. I declined because I didn't want to make the compromises I saw others make.

I didn't take the time to learn why. I didn't consider the impact on my community with my decision.

Unearthing Prevailing Ideas

I read a lot for my own entertainment, and I read a lot for my spiritual growth. Occasionally, I read something like Isabel Wilkerson's *The Warmth of Other Suns* and learned in depth about a history I had only glossed over before. Once I understood that the years of slavery were not just oriented in the South and that the North benefited greatly, I had to change my mind about avoiding the South all my life as the eternal "evil empire."

Once I understood the details of the great migration of Blacks from the South to the North and how they continued to be oppressed, I had to acknowledge in a deeper way the systems that worked against people who looked like me. I likely escaped some impact because my mother chose to keep us away from Black culture and influences, moving us into white schools and neighborhoods.

Up until this moment, I had not learned or deeply inquired about how my upbringing shaped my view of the world. Learning about the world includes learning about my own place in it. Learning about what ideas and beliefs drive my behavior was the beginning of understanding my place, my contribution.

As part of my independent work, once I left the corporate arena, I learned how to facilitate Rayona Sharpnack's Contextual Leadership workshop series. Her book, *Trade Up; Reinventing Leadership from the Inside Out*, gives a full explanation of the workshop process, but I want to share some of the central ideas here.

I learned from her about "prevailing ideas" or "context" that drive our behavior. I was in my early forties when I grasped this concept. Going through one of the exercises, I unearthed the prevailing idea, "I didn't deserve my success because I hadn't brought along with me enough people who looked like me." I was often the only woman, the only Black person, or the only identified lesbian in the room.

I reconciled my feelings of shame and guilt by trading up to the idea that "as I am lifted, others are lifted." It was a good shift, and it made me feel better about my success. It encouraged me to pursue more. However, I didn't go back and look to see if others were lifted. It was convenient to say I was lifted and to believe it rather than witness it.

I had a shift in attitude, but what had I actually learned?

As I continued to rise in the corporate ranks and in income, I was vaguely aware of the ever-increasing gap in resources. I could see unhoused people in California, where I lived fifty of my now sixty-six years. I could see how home prices and rents soared. But I was comfortable.

I sold a house at a loss to take a job at lower pay helping pass school bonds to repair and improve schools. I felt redeemed for that year but went back to the corporate world to make the big bucks again. I learned why the schools were underfunded, but I gave up on overturning the proposition that caused the most harm.

Finding Relative Peace Within

I listed as one of my confessions that I wanted to avoid conflict. I think it's more accurate to say that I wanted to avoid uncertainty. I assiduously avoided anything that might rock my current beliefs, with the exception of spiritual beliefs that I thought might free me from my suffering and guilt. I had a position, a point of view. I was a successful Black, lesbian woman. My success was hard earned and well deserved.

Because I was capable, I had to perform. It was my obligation and my privilege. I needed to do the right thing at all times. I needed to please whoever I perceived as having power over me.

As I was going through my life from age nineteen into my forties, I was raising three children. I can't remember reading more than a couple of books that related to parenting. I wasn't willing to learn that I probably was doing it all wrong. I needed to stay certain that I was successful and doing my best.

When our son was troubled in his teens and heading toward residential therapy, the family therapist asked us, "Are you willing to consider that you two 'high-fire' people have a 'low-fire' son?" We categorically rejected this idea. It didn't fit comfortably with our plans for our lives and his. We were unwilling to learn how to support who he might be rather than who we wanted him to be.

Twice in my life I made weak suicide attempts, the first time by ingesting twenty-seven Excedrin tablets, the second time by taking a handful of sleeping pills. These were weak attempts because I immediately told someone nearby in both cases in order to be rescued. They were really cries for attention.

It turns out the attention I wanted was my own attention to who I truly was. What was my authentic self longing to express? What was instead being repressed by my addiction to accomplishment and getting a good grade?

For such a long time, I was unwilling to learn who I was inside. I had to learn what made me so sad. When I saw video of myself in my twenties with my three children, I did not recognize my own spirit. I remember watching, thinking, "Who was she, this sad young woman?"

It took leaving two marriages and decades of every type of therapy to arrive at a place of relative peace within myself. But this peace includes an open heart. And the open heart leads to questioning how deeply and widely I love the world. And this open heart teaches me responsibility for so much more than myself or my constellation.

What We Know and What We Don't

There is a powerful program I witnessed once called "Facing History and Ourselves." I remember how much impact it had on participants. One aspect of the program was hearing the facts of major events in history and relating them to how we act in similar situations now. The program taught empathy, curiosity, and civic responsibility.

One example showed viewers a picture of the Black Panthers in the 1960s and asked them to recall what they thought they knew about them. Many of my own recollections were radical, violent, resistors, protestors, against the system. But I had no details. As the instructor pointed out what many forgot: the lunch programs for students, the mentoring, the cultural pride events that the Black Panthers founded and shared. I was sad. I was sad that I didn't know or take the time to know what they were really trying to do. Learning enough could have shaped a different path and approach to life for me.

The missed opportunities for learning about the world I live in —the neighborhood, the region, the state, the country—leave me ill equipped to form an opinion based on facts. I can know right from wrong, but only if I understand what actually happened or is happening. Getting the full picture takes a lot of study.

History is written by those who have the privilege to write. To understand the full picture, you have to seek out alternative versions, frequently hidden or ignored, and then come to conclusions for yourself.

I am aware that war has been part of the human experience for millennia. I am aware that men were not always the leaders in society. I am aware that Indigenous peoples have wisdom about how to live on the Earth in a harmonious way.

But I was unaware of so much. For example, our family always talked about being Cherokee. It wasn't until a member of my broader family tree did the work to investigate that we learned we were not born of the Cherokee tribe, but we were enslaved by the Cherokee tribe. Our great grandfather was listed on the rolls as a "Cherokee freedman."

After the Emancipation Proclamation, we became part of the nation. Does that mean the Cherokee wisdom is not valid? No. It means there is more to the story of what their values were. It means

I don't have an all-or-nothing view of the inherent "goodness" of all things Indigenous.

Then when someone has a different idea of how the First People should be treated, I am more informed of the full story. I can hold two things at once. They were mistreated and wronged—and they mistreated and were wrong.

Comfort At All Costs

Today when I am in a discussion with someone about the problems I see with the current federal administration in the United States, my lack of learning is a disability. I can list all my grievances, including how Ukraine is being treated. But in this case, the person I was speaking to asked if I knew what NATO previously promised to Russia. I had no idea. While the history wouldn't excuse behavior, I might have more credibility to elicit compassion for Ukraine if I understood a fuller story. I need to be open to learning, even if I stay consistent to my values.

The conspiracy theorists in my constellation turned out to be right about a lot of things. I followed along about the consolidation of power in our country, the consolidation of media, the consolidation of wealth. I followed along but didn't raise the alarm.

I learned so much about the food industry and the diabolical greed that makes our nation sick. I shared what I learned, but not loudly, not consistently. I recognized the pharmaceutical industry as not trustworthy, but I allowed them access to my body anyway. It was easier, somehow more comfortable, to know but tuck it away and not dwell on what I knew.

I remained comfortable in my understanding of the world for decades. It is comfortable to believe the country you live in is better than most, even if it's not true. It's comfortable to write checks instead of taking a deeper look at the problem. Its comfortable to hang out with people who agree with your ideas so you never really have to test them.

Christie Hardwick

- *I didn't learn enough. To understand the geopolitical landscape is to act responsibly. You can't take informed action without being informed.*
- *I didn't want to face conflict.*
- *I didn't want to believe the conspiracy theorists.*
- *I was comfortable.*

4

The Goal of Staying Proximate

- *I didn't do enough.*
- *I voted. I made a few calls.*
- *I didn't act with urgency or consistency.*
- *I had a list of excuses for not doing.*

I START this chapter by moaning. I say to myself, "You just wrote a book that says basically love is all there is, and it is your ultimate assignment." Yes, I did. And I stand by that idea. Loving deep and wide is why we are here.

And love is an action word. Love in motion, love as a basis for my behavior. Learning to love in greater and greater ways. Not bigger but more inclusively, more totally, more unconditionally.

As humans living together, we can constantly evolve our ability to love. Since I have chosen to be in the world and not on a mountaintop, I know there are contributions I can make. Prayer, meditation, and good vibrations do matter—a lot.

Dwelling in love and focusing on love are the ways to prepare the soil for great things to emerge. Practicing the presence of love wherever we are strengthens our ability to be love in every situation.

Spiritual practices matter. And in this human experience, these practices are not the totality of my expression on this planet at this time. Devotion can coexist with action.

You might say, "You've lived sixty-six years, and in that time, if I look at your resume, you've done a lot." I will admit to significant

37

accomplishments. Its not as if I've done nothing or no thing of importance. I have. I raised three wonderful people. I did meaningful volunteer work. I did good creative work. I contributed to the capacity of my clients to do their great work. I loved to the best of my ability, and I'm getting better.

Where I fall short, and the reason for this book, is the activity taken on behalf of the whole, with recognition and awareness of the effect you intend to have. The intention is key. You may choose to focus all your attention on gardening or raising bees. If it's done with the intention to benefit all, that in itself makes it more powerful.

I confess to living most of my life being good for the sake of my own soul and not for the sake of others. I have grown in that these past ten years, but I have such a long way to go. I wrote this after the public murder of George Floyd: I want my friends, allies, and those who care to take up this mantra "I want to live in a world where *you* feel safe and loved." This is what I wanted, demanded from those activated by his on-the-ground lynching: I wanted them to *do* something and *say* something that demonstrated they were dedicated to such a world. I wanted them to really want me to feel safe and loved. I wanted them to care and learn and act appropriately. What would the world look like if each of us wanted for everyone a world where they feel safe and loved? What would we need to be doing?

What It Means to Stay Proximate

I admire and revere Bryan Stevenson for his character and his work. The Equal Justice Institute, its venues and programs are a continuation of the legacy of the Civil Rights Movement. I am in awe of what he has built on the rise of a hill in Montgomery, Alabama. I have visited the Legacy Museum twice and will be moved to go again. I joined a local chapter of his work when I lived in Florida, and while it was challenging, it was meaningful. What

Stevenson admonishes every time he speaks, is to "get proximate" with that which we want to understand and that which we desire to change.

As a Harvard trained lawyer instead of going the lucrative route of a big firm, he ended up getting proximate with prisoners on death row in Alabama. He has dedicated his life to caring, protecting, lifting, and freeing these abandoned people whenever possible. He also has connected their experiences to all of our experiences.

He attracts people of all ethnic backgrounds and social statuses and politics to be part of demanding and working toward equal justice. He's done it with teaching and with shocking. The memorial to all the documented lynchings in this country shocks and teaches. As you walk through the copper columns inscribed with the county and the names of those who were hung from trees, you have to feel the magnitude and the reality of it.

The experience of being at the museum and the memorial in Alabama moved me to find people doing the work of "Confronting the Legacy of Racial Terror" where I lived. The Equal Justice Initiative, founded by Stevenson, leads these efforts through its Community Remembrance Project. The idea was that we needed to care about those terrorized, understand why they were terrorized, and understand the lasting impacts of that terror so we could take meaningful action in our community today.

I joined the local group. I even took on a leadership role. I stumbled through creating bylaws, clarifying our purpose and many Zoom calls during the pandemic to gain a greater understanding of how recognizing lynchings that happened on the neighborhood's soil could help us be better now. The meetings were painfully disorganized, filled with drama and not always productive, but I hung in there to be proximate.

This was the first time in my decades of living where I was working primarily with Black people on Black history and the current effects of racism. I got involved with a ministers' association founded by Black ministers, supported the local Black History

Museum, and became integrated into the Black community. I did this for a couple of years, until my mate and I decided to move from Florida back to California.

I left and, other than a few continuing donations, have not continued the work. I felt sad to leave the work, and I felt selfish to move on, but I did it anyway. I think about the people there who could also leave but choose to stay and do the work and the people who can't leave, whom I abandoned.

People Who Chart the Path

I have many examples of people in my life—close enough to love, touch, and have lasting friendships with—who showed me the way of doing enough. While I supported each of them in their contributions, I did not step up in the ways they have.

Kevin Jennings founded the Gay, Lesbian, Straight Education Network out of his experiences and the suffering of young LGBTQ+ students when he was a teacher. From this impactful organization, he went on to lead time and again and to be a force for change in the world. He never truly rests. He credits me with being a wonderful guide for him; I credit him for giving my life more meaning.

I met Dr. LaDonna Butler after watching her facilitate a circle in the middle of the street in a Black neighborhood in South St. Petersburg, Florida. The neighborhood had experienced gun violence, and she sought to help people understand what was happening and what to do about it. I heard youth describe why they carried weapons. I heard elders cry about how they didn't know how to speak to youth. I heard parents, exhausted, looking for alternatives for their children's energies, dreams, and desires. Dr. Butler walks the walk every day, helping people navigate mental health and wellness personally and collectively.

My friend Jane Bunker moved from Cape Cod, Massachusetts, to St. Petersburg, Florida, when she was in her seventies and tapped right into the African American Museum there. She is a renown artist and painted at least one hundred paintings over several years, auctioning them off to start a scholarship fund for promising Black youth. The scholarship fund continues years later with support from many sectors of the city. She's done so much, and she is not stopping as she celebrates her eightieth birthday now. She and her husband, Mason, are forces for good.

My friend Melissa Sawyer has dedicated twenty years of her life to empowering youth in New Orleans. She's a Canadian migrant who came to help after Hurricane Katrina and saw the suffering of the local community (primarily Black). She stayed, and she served, and she changed lives.

My friend Selisse Berry came out as lesbian and was rejected to be a minister after completing seminary. Instead of licking her wounds, she started an organization called Out & Equal so no one else would have to choose between work they love and who they love. She started with an idea and, with determination, grew it to be a movement. The movement for workplace equality brought thousands of people and hundreds of corporations together to make workplaces safer and the beneficiaries of engaged employees.

Every person I mentioned in my acknowledgments at the front of this book has a story of caring, learning, and acting that contributes to improving the lives of others. I am forever grateful for their presence in my life. They inspired me, and yet I remained a leader who often did not lead.

Sometimes I have taken action, done enough, but with blinders on.

The Lure and Let Down of Politics

When we had what looked like a great chance to elect our first woman to be President of the United States—Hillary Clinton—I rolled up my sleeves and closed my mind to any other outcome. When Bernie Sanders complained about being shut out, I thought, "Here's another old white man complaining when he doesn't get the top slot." When I heard that unfair things were done at the party level to shut him out, I justified it with the end that I hoped for.

I made countless calls and donations and worked to get out the vote. In the end, I acted but without an open mind. I was wrong about Bernie Sanders. He had a great following, and I should have given him consideration. I could have still chosen Hillary, but my actions would have been fully informed.

I didn't want to be informed. I wanted the outcome I wanted. How can I say my behavior is different from the MAGA people now?

When Barack Obama was the candidate, I also initially wanted our first female president. But once he won the nomination, I was all in.

By the time of Donald Trump's first election, I was terribly disappointed, but I didn't dive right into the necessary action, the action that needed to be sustained to keep his agenda in check. I knew Trump's agenda was problematic, but I went back to my life, writing an occasional check and maybe one or two letters to my Congressional representatives. I wasn't willing to disrupt my life by treating politics as a part of my daily, weekly, monthly responsibilities.

I let things unfold, occasionally complaining and often resting on my laurels while Joe Biden and Kamala Harris were in office, even if it was clear their policies needed improvement across the board. I could see that we should hold them accountable and demand explanations and more effort, but I instead spent time making Facebook posts and buying from Amazon.

My daily life consisted of taking care of my body with exercise and food, assiduously studying both. I also devoted time daily to spiritual practices, reading, writing, listening, and learning. Every week, I spent time with friends or family, keeping connections strong. Every week, I worked as a leadership coach and supported people doing important work. Every week, I indulged in entertainment and shopping. Every month or so, I traveled near or far in search of ever more enjoyable experiences.

What my daily life did not consist of was educating myself about the local and global world that I was living in. I did not read the local or regional newspaper. I did not attend to any political action weekly or monthly. I didn't write or call government representatives to weigh in on how they were voting or what they were not proposing or their plans for moving forward. I put no pressure on and provided no input to local, state, or federal governments. I wrote checks and occasionally volunteered or attended a meeting about social issues, but I was inconsistent at best.

I Didn't Do Enough

Earlier I spoke about my extensive experience in education. I understood how it worked and what was broken in it. My twin children both work in education, as does one of their spouses. They work hard and struggle in a system that is underfunded and over regulated. Their hands are tied when it comes to doing what's best for children. Parental and state expectations exceed the resources allocated.

I was part of the leadership decades before that should have done more about it and stayed on it until we did. Now, when the current administration has people trying to move from public to private, from desegregated to segregated, from acknowledging different languages to ignoring them, to making school safety a bottom of the list priority, I can be held accountable for not doing more to protect and improve what we had.

I didn't do enough to usher in a different outcome than what we are experiencing today. I didn't act enough. I voted. I made some calls. But I didn't act with urgency and visibility or consistency.

With so many causes I cared about—the climate, refugees, LGBTQ+, Black Lives Matter, youth empowerment, homelessness, child trafficking, nature conservation, reproductive freedom, and the list goes on—I became a checkbook philanthropist.

Checkbook activism isn't nothing, but it also is not enough.

Christie Hardwick

I didn't stay proximate. I might have been proximate, and then I left as soon as possible.

- *I didn't do enough.*
- *I voted. I made a few calls.*
- *I didn't act with urgency or consistency.*
- *I had a list of excuses for not doing.*

5

Spirituality Informs
Our Human Experience

- *I had tools to get out of any discomfort.*
- *I had spiritual ideas to shield me.*
- *I leaned on spiritual practices to transcend pain.*
- *I relied on love and an open heart as solution.*
- *Like Lennon, I hoped "they" would join me.*

I AM grateful I have spiritual practices and a spiritual philosophy that hold my life together. Without a belief in something greater than my body, blood, and brains, I don't think I'd be long for this world. The perspective that I am part of universal source energy, imbued with Divine intelligence, connected to all of life in consciousness gives me a basis from which to operate.

Since I believe each of us matters to the whole, I am taking this inventory to benefit myself, my growth and awareness, and on behalf of everyone whose life I touch. Being able to meditate and center on peace within, being able to focus on and find light in every situation, being able to respond to whatever I encounter with an open heart makes this life worth living.

All that being true for me, I also have used my spiritually to avoid pain. The things I didn't care enough about and didn't learn enough about, I could wave a wand of prayer over and not feel the devastation of the human condition. Don't get me wrong, I do not think staying in perpetual suffering or pain on behalf of others is the way to live. I just realize you cannot avoid it altogether and be whole.

Before accepting that love and good will ultimately prevail, I must feel my despair. I must say: I feel sick. I feel pain. I feel a depth of sorrow. I feel fear.

Being human is hard. Even if we see ourselves as Spirit having a human experience, the human experience is hard. We can do hard, but we have to go through it, not around it or above it.

I admit to transcending world conditions regularly. I imagine this will always be necessary for me. I cannot hold the pain or sorrow for too long without being paralyzed by it. I have to transcend and rest, but I have to go back into it.

My temptation is to stay "above" it all, with my Mona Lisa smile, and lead others out of the wilderness of suffering. This is actually my role, but I can't always stay there or I lose my ability to understand the human condition.

Spiritual Beings Having a Human Experience

I see that in both science and spirituality, energy cannot be destroyed. Therefore, in some form, all of us continue. This is spiritually comforting and could be relied on to avoid the sorrow of loss in human experience. Some may do this, but I do not ascribe to it. Even if we are eternal as energetic beings, this trip on the planet is finite. We are limited in the body.

I have come to think that as spiritual beings, we chose the experience we are having so as to grow our understanding of life. Even if this is so, it hurts to be ill, to lose others, and to experience the withholding of love. We experience darkness here on Earth, and it is more than the night and more than the absence of light.

I know many do not believe as I do and may never entertain the thought of an eternal soul or a divine origin. I cannot rely on people thinking as I do or doing as I do as a solution.

People have to be met where they are, and I have to accept that my message of openheartedness and love is not for everyone. I have to realize that some need me to sit with them in the darkness until they are willing to consider the existence of light. I cannot ask them to know what they don't know or see what they don't see. I can only witness and be present as a form of love. I cannot use spirituality to avoid pain.

Experience Mirrors Thoughts

I recently ran across an influencer on Instagram who said something to the effect of freedom is not comfort, and comfort is sedation. It makes sense to me that sometimes we have to be uncomfortable. Always striving for comfort keeps us locked in a cycle of consuming, avoiding, numbing, and suppressing. When something upsets me, I can consume food or entertainment. I don't use alcohol anymore, but I do numb myself with immersive experiences that block out the present circumstances.

In one sense, I enjoy the moment, the beautiful dish prepared for me, the engaging book or movie, but it matters how I approach it and when. Do I reach for something when I begin to feel my despair or sorrow? Do I suppress it in order to have a different experience?

Many wise people have said that disease has a lot to do with suppressed emotions. I continually work on feeling safe to feel. There is part of me that thinks if I feel too much, I'll never get back control of my emotions. Instead, they will take me to a place of no return. I believe that thought arises because I've preemptively practiced meditation and breathwork more than I've practiced feeling my emotions and navigating my way back to peace. Some of these ideas come from the teaching I studied, Science of the Mind. Our minds, our consciousness is so powerful that it is constantly creating experiences that match the pattern of our thoughts. Not our actual thoughts (e.g., an elephant doesn't appear because I've thought of one) but the pattern of my thoughts being optimistic, pessimistic, hopeful, despairing, trusting, or fearful. My experience mirrors the pattern of my thoughts.

I constantly dwell on love as the ultimate idea, and I experience a lot of love in my life—not just in my constellation but also people who are kind to me in everyday exchanges. Even when I am in Italy struggling with the language, people help me in small ways consistently. I think this comes from their big hearts, but it is also my thoughts drawing people like that into my orbit. And my thoughts of love, peace and good resonate with them and bring out their best behavior.

These experiences sometimes make me think that everyone can change their patterns and change the world. And while I think that is ultimately true, I also can't ignore the evidence of people thinking in fearful, judgmental, and even hateful ways. I must acknowledge the existence and impact of destructive thought patterns and keep my own patterns based in love.

I must continue to use my spiritual tools, as for now they keep me getting up and facing each day. I need meditation. I need breathwork. I need tree hugging, music, singing, laughing, and community. I need to rest in the arms of a greater idea, every day.

But I cannot use spirituality to avoid pain. The pain is a message. It says, "Respond to this. Do what is yours to do."

- *I used spirituality to avoid pain.*
- *I had tools to get out of any discomfort.*
- *I had spiritual ideas to shield me.*
- *I leaned on spiritual practices to transcend.*
- *I relied on love and an open heart as solution,*
- *Like Lennon, I hoped "they" would join me.*

6

The Impact, the Consequences

THE IMPACT OF NOT CARING, learning, or acting enough turns out to result in predictable outcomes. The outcomes are predictable because we begin to think in a loop, staying on the same path of ideas. We think in ways that are comfortable and fit the narrative we've ascribed to in our minds. We chose to filter out anything that challenges our thinking so that we can have some measure of peace, however superficial.

This is easier than questioning our worldview when something comes up against it. It is easier to look for something that fits and look away from that which forces us to reconsider. It rarely occurred to me to watch the news the "other side" watches, to read what they read.

I recently did just that and was amazed at how logical the writers presented ideas I thought were dangerous or crazy sounding. I had new-found empathy for those who held views of the world different from my own. This is a new development, as I spent most of my adult life staying in my bubble.

In the early 1990s, I worked on Bill Clinton's presidential campaign. I remember being mesmerized by his charisma. Once he took the time to see me when he shook my hand in a clump of people surrounding and clamoring for him. He had my hand and kept it until he could look in my eyes for a moment and greet me.

When all the stories of his philandering came out, I remember thinking, "Oh well. He's a man." Once you get on the train with a person and an idea, in this case the man from Hope, you stay in your seat.

When the Clintons left out the congressman in my district when they drafted their version of a universal health care plan, I didn't stand up for him and make myself heard. He had worked tirelessly for more than a decade and had a great understanding of the nuances required to successfully alter our nation's approach to health care.

The Clinton health plan failed, but I stayed on the train. I stayed on the train when Monica Lewinsky came out with her dirty dress. I disparaged her, asking, "Who saves a dirty dress?" He was my guy, so whatever he did could be excused.

From one Clinton to the other, I stayed in my seat on that train. I felt George W. Bush was not my president. I couldn't and wouldn't understand the people who elected him. I remember being in a room where he was addressing a women's leadership group I was part of. When Colin Powell came out first, I immediately shot out of my seat and gave him respect. When Bush came out, I leaned half way up out of my chair and sat back down.

I wasn't even curious what positive attributes he might have. He hardly existed for me. After 9/11, when he called for us to show our patriotism by shopping and then Congress passed the Patriots Act that changed forever our personal privacy, I wasn't paying any attention.

Consequences.

Isolated in My Own Bubble

This sense of separation kept me isolated in my liberal bubble, living in California and the Bay Area—in San Francisco, Sunnyvale, Mountain View, Campbell, and Santa Clara. It was mostly an echo chamber of, "We are about people, they just care about money." I bought the idea that Democrats were all about social programs and Republicans about fiscal responsibility. I missed that in votes and laws and actual improved lives of people, the parties were often equally ineffective.

Today we have a party in power that is actually destructive.

People like me paved their way by being indifferent and rigid. When their followers were confused and scared by gender identity and expression, I did not give them grace. Nor was I given grace when I mistakenly used the wrong pronoun for someone.

It was like being in the know or being outside the family circle. Those who named the Indigenous land they stood on, those who placed their pronouns under their name on Zoom, were paragons of cultural enlightenment.

Those who didn't were judged for being behind the times at best and transphobic, white supremacists, or colonists at worst. This is not to say that these efforts to be inclusive of gender identity and to acknowledge indigenous land were not justified or beneficial, but it is to say that teaching, showing, sharing, and giving grace also have a place. The lack of grace has had consequences.

On this point, I must also say that those who advocate for making trans people disappear, promote death for gay people in other parts of the world, and who deny massacres of Indigenous peoples and their stolen land are not having just a difference of opinion. They are dismissing truth and humans as not worthy of life.

Owning my rigidity is not owning that I should understand or tolerate people who want someone like me or my transgender friends not to exist. That which invites violence and bullying and even death needs to be called out, always.

Sometimes when I am unsure about sources or facts, instead of researching and taking a stand and risking judgment, ridicule, or abandonment, I'll stay quiet. For example, I did not share a post about a transgender man who was kidnapped and brutally raped and murdered. I did not want to associate with it, in case there was something I did not know.

What else could I possibly need to know? Why wouldn't I post his picture on my timeline the way I posted about volunteering to help children learn how to read? Because I know the teaching/reading post uplifts my followers without upsetting anyone. Is it my role not to upset anyone? How fragile I behave when its uncomfortable. That man's life, just like George Floyd's life, needed to be acknowledged by everyone who learned of it.

Five years before the overturn of Roe v. Wade, I was having a conversation with a neighbor. We were generally talking about the state of our country, and she stated that women's reproductive rights were in danger. She cited cases that were cropping up in different states and said they were precursors to making abortion illegal again.

I remember casually saying, "There are no reports of this. I think you exaggerate. I wouldn't want to spread fear about something that might not be even happening." This happened during Trump's first term, and I had decided he was a blip, a retaliation for having had a successful first Black president. My neighbor asked, "Are you going to wait until a woman dies in a back alley before you investigate this?"

Much later I poured money into Planned Parenthood and reproductive rights advocacy groups, but it was too late.

Consequences.

The Cost of Withheld Compassion

Recently, I walked about a half a mile between my hotel and the Italian Consulate in San Francisco. By the time I reached my destination, I was sobbing. Shocked by the number of unhoused people who were waking up, moving their makeshift sleeping quarters, the city workers who were washing the streets of excrement, the unshaven, haggard, dirty faces that peered at me briskly walking, my hands in my pockets, my head slightly down, my eyes averted. I could not fix this. I could not reach into my purse and pull out dollars and help. I could not say anything that would help.

I conducted my business and walked on a different street on the way back. As I did that day, I can choose to keep separate from them by not seeing the devastation of hope in their faces when I pass by, as they wonder, "Does she care? Does she see me? I am a man! I am a woman! I am someone!"

As I recall this, I cannot find the same tears that ravaged me. I rarely cry, and the sobs took me by surprise. When I arrived at the Consulate, still openingly weeping, a security guard looked at me tenderly and said, "It's rough out there." He had compassion for me, compassion for my compassion.

The contrast was sobering. I hadn't said a word to the people whose circumstances made me weep.

Consequences.

Facing the Grief

The rareness of tears has consequences. As I take this inventory and recognize where I can step up in my life and where I need to forgive myself, I also must pay attention to the grief I feel. The grief can be masked with rage, anger, and defiance, but it is grief all the same.

I am deeply sad about conditions in our society. I am deeply sad because the conditions exist *and* because I can't fix them. I need to face my grief and feel the pain of it and let it transform into emotion I can act from. There is no shortcut to this.

I kept myself from feeling deeply for so long that it is very hard to find my tears. Without the depth of tears, I also limit the height of joy. Without shedding tears, I teach my family to be stoic, even though I don't believe it's healthy. They look to me as the matriarch to show the way.

There is always someone looking to you to see how to navigate. I want to show a healthy, lighter way—a way that has been watered with real tears and the growth that came from surviving the dark nights. Without feeling the depth of my sorrow I limit the life I experience and I limit the compassion I have for others.

Consequences.

The Price of Not Engaging

Another impact of not taking time to investigate and learn is to become desensitized by all I hear. Every day, especially during the Trump administration, I get texts from Democrats who are sounding the alarm, using what come across as scare tactics or false hope" We are impeaching Trump! Social Security is gone! You are at risk! Did you switch parties? We don't see your vote on putting criminal charges on DOGE!

All the messages end by asking for money. So I treat them all the same and decide when I'll send money based on how sincere I think the plea is. I don't look up information to see if impeachment proceedings are real or if criminal charges are being filed. If I did I could decide which things to support based on facts, but I'm busy with everything else and randomly send $27 to the most compelling message. Is the National Governors Association better than the Democratic National Committee? Is an individual candidate flipping a seat blue better than supporting town halls across the country?

Since I haven't taken the time to learn what is most effective in stopping the destruction and what is most effective in helping real people, I take a shot in the dark, trusting that *someone* is doing the right thing. I also could contact those writing and let them know that their alarmist messaging isn't working for me, but I might learn it works for most.

My greatest, most used excuse for not engaging on all the topics is, "It's too much. I can't say something about everything. I need to share what gives hope, what brings light, what inspires." I have not questioned whether only sharing light is in service to others or to my fear of rejection.

I believe in all the light I share. I believe putting my attention primarily on what I want to see, attracts more of it into my experience *and* I believe I become more deeply human when I feel what hurts. One of the things that hurts is how I haven't responded to the pain I see with compassionate, direct, and proximate actions.

The impact of all this was a sense of separation, not feeling connected to all of humanity, believing for periods of time that I was an island.

I went on with my life, knowing things were getting worse for my children and grandchildren. I did not consistently speak up when things were wrong, whether coming from the right or the left.

So here I am having to take accountability for the outcome: Our nation threatened by indifference while its democratic ideals are destroyed, one by one—the rule of law, due process, dignity of the presidency, the global alliances, the work for peace, humanitarian aid. And even if it were imperfectly executed, we still once were a place that celebrated freedom and progress. Not now.

Consequences.

7

Remorse Requires
Self-Forgiveness

- *I should have listened when my neighbor said reproductive rights were under attack.*
- *That situation times one hundred may have prodded me to acting sooner, to sound the alarm sooner. I am sorry.*
- *I went on with my life, knowing things were getting worse for my children and grandchildren.*
- *This is my grief.*
- *This is my conundrum.*

REMORSE. So much I'm sorry for and need to forgive. Remorse. They say regrets are not useful, but I have them anyway. I am sorry I didn't use the gift of intelligence and spoken and written word to lift up my community sooner and better. I must forgive myself so I can garner the energy to move forward.

My remorse centers on staying superficial when things became too uncomfortable, on not speaking out when I knew better, and on my total lack of curiosity about others.

I wrote earlier about activist, lawyer, and philanthropist Bryan Stevenson encouraging and admonishing us to get proximate. I've been afraid to get too close to big problems, fearing I'll be consumed by them and lose myself in the process. I supported some leaders who suffer from racism, heterosexism, sexism, and general bullying. I also work with leaders who run complex organizations designed to solve complex social problems.

I prepare myself to be their witness and provide guidance to get them through their days. But they are the ones dealing directly with the big problems they are trying to solve. They are the ones who are proximate with the social ill and the devastating consequences. I am one step removed and can breathe through my discomfort and move on to the next person. While this is a valuable service, it keeps me in my head and often puts my heart on pause.

If I were to feel what they are feeling, I might not be able to help. Vietnamese monk Thich Nhât Hạnh said, "Someone asked me, 'Aren't you worried about the state of the world?' I allowed myself to breathe, and then I said, 'What is most important is not to allow your anxiety about what happens in the world to fill your heart. If your heart is filled with anxiety, you will get sick and you will not be able to help.'"

Another way I've heard that said is to observe but not absorb.

I subscribe to the wise monk's idea. Yet I regret that it keeps me from feeling more deeply. I have chosen the work I do and haven't allowed myself periods of grieving or sadness or rage. They all arise, and I use my spiritual sword to cut them down. This has contributed to my sense of separation. I may know we are all connected, but I don't always experience it.

Finding My Path to Self-Forgiveness

Where there is remorse, there needs to be forgiveness. There are so many things in life I would have done differently had I known better or had more capacity at the time. Here I lean on the wisdom of Dr. Maya Angelou: "Do the best you can until you know better. Then when you know better, do better."

I am actively in the process of forgiving myself. The book I wrote in 2023, *Radical-Self Tenderness*, guides me toward less harsh, gentler internal judgment. If I move through forgiveness, I can move on more clearly to what is mine to do now.

In this book to this point, I wrote nearly 10,000 words describing my shortcomings. I am well aware that I could write the same about what my best looked like and where it did good. This book is for another purpose, though, so I must stay on point. I need to look at the uncomfortable to stretch my comfort zone, I need to say I'm sorry for all I could not see or do. This self-awareness is not to give myself a beating but to arrive at a place to begin anew.

I've listed just a few of the times when I didn't listen. Just a few of the times when I could have learned more. Just a few of the times when I stuck to my narrative and would not consider another one.

Another thing I want to forgive myself for is my lack of curiosity about other people, partly because I get bored telling my own story, so I presume others do, too. But some of it is that I don't want to know you too well. I don't want to open my heart to yet another human. Because it turns out that a lot of you are easy to love, and if I get curious about more of you, I'll love more of you. And I have yet to know what to do with all of that.

I'm a work in progress, and I'm beginning to understand that extending interest and being curious are in themselves sometimes enough. Being seen by another can lift our spirits and make a difference about how we feel in our lives in that moment.

When I ask questions and listen to stories, I meet extraordinary humans. And I need to be OK with heart-wide-open conversations that lead to no further connection, like when I'm in an airport or on a plane, having a conversattion and then going our separate ways. I have never regretted a conversation I had. I have always regretted those that occurred to me but that I ignored and didn't initiate.

I forgive my unwillingness to be curious.

Taking My Inventory

I forgive myself for not consciously building social action into my daily life—and for not knowing how I should do that or what it should look like or even whether how I'm living now is sufficient. I just didn't consider it as important as my personal health, the health of my personal relationships, and the health of my extended constellation of people including those I work with. I'm not even sure I need to build social action into my daily life and I wonder if the attention I give to my constellation is beneficial enough to warrant feeling OK about myself.

But I am now willing to give it a hard look and determine the way forward for now. I say for now because I must continue to learn and grow as must we all.

These words may or may not resonate with you, depending on where you are on your own path. But if they do, come with me the rest of the way.

I will describe a way forward that lets me process what I didn't care enough about, learn enough about, and do enough about. If every person could stop and take inventory of how they live in relation to the social good, I believe that to be a worthwhile exercise. How should I care? What should I care about? What do I need to learn? How should I learn? What do I need to do? How should I do it?

This reminds me of the wonderful Shakespeare class I took from Tina Packard. She said that in everything Shakespeare wrote, he asked and answered three questions: What does it mean to be alive? How shall we act? What must I do?

Remorse necessitates forgiveness.

- *I should have listened when my neighbor said reproductive rights were under attack.*
- *That situation times one hundred may have prodded me to acting sooner, to sound the alarm sooner. I am sorry.*
- *I went on with my life, knowing things were getting worse for my children and grandchildren.*
- *This is my grief.*
- *This is my conundrum.*

8

The Way Forward

- *What to be and do now?*
- *Radical self-tenderness?*
- *To what end—loving deep and wide?*

I STILL BELIEVE IN, stand in these ideas. But what else?

Do I continue to believe in radical self-tenderness? Absolutely. Being violent with myself would only contribute to violence in the world. At this moment, I tenderly approach a new way of living, a new level of engagement.

Do I continue to believe we are here to love both deep and wide? Absolutely. I am learning the nuances of the fierceness of love—the aspect that had Jesus turn over the gambling tables in the temple; the perseverant love of Nelson Mandela that kept him imprisoned for twenty-seven years; the sacrificed lives of Martin, Bobby, and John; the deepness of love that calls me to speak truth to power on behalf of the whole.

The way forward calls us to do a lot less othering, a lot less believing groups of people are intrinsically different from us.

There are too many situations where the mantra involves "them" and "us." The way forward means paying attention when I distance myself from another human because they are not my tribe. I've read that this is a natural human tendency, to be tribal. And I can choose to override this ancestral trait.

I had the opportunity to do just that when I was being followed by a man on a quiet street in an Italian neighborhood. I saw him pass me in his car, then I noticed him pass me again. I was walking slowly, looking at homes, just taking a leisurely walk. It was sunny out, and I was wearing a simple sleeveless sundress and a straw hat.

The third time I saw him, he stopped the car, got out, and began to speak to me in Italian, smiling. I cocked my head trying to understand, but I was very early in my language acquisition and couldn't quite make out if he was asking for help or wanted me to get in the car. Because I didn't understand, I smiled back and said, "No, thank you." He blew me a kiss and made a gesture with his hand. And then I understood. He was asking me to come with him, thinking I was available for sex, that I was a prostitute.

I recently learned that several women who happened to be from Nigeria had been selling sex on the side of local roads. I was brown-skinned, so he extrapolated.

At first I was shook up. Then I was angry. Then I saw the light.

I judged those women. I saw myself as above them. How could he think that of me! Does he know who I am and what I've accomplished? Does he know how I live and how many resources are at my disposal?

After my inner dialogue, a peace settled in me. Oh, I think I could never be in the position of those women. I think they must have missed some set of directions or opportunities that led them to find themselves in this position. In reality, I had no idea. I did not know if they were desperate sex workers, or if they chose it without judgment. I did not know if they were being exploited, or if they were exploiting themselves.

I decided based on what? I let go of my feeling of offense and was left with the feeling of having been mistaken for someone else, without the emotional charge of wounded pride.

Seeing Ourselves in the Others

I have presumed a lot about people who chose to vote Republican in 2024 and who cheer on the behavior of the Trump administration. I put these voters all in the same bucket, not different from

Hillary Clinton's famous "basket of deplorables." I presume I'm smarter, more educated, more worldly than they. But the fact is, I don't know.

Just like I don't want people to treat me based on a stereotype they hold or what they think they know by looking at me, I didn't have the right to treat every person who was on the other side of the political spectrum as if they were a stereotype. It's easier to blame them than to understand how to design and implement a society that works for all of us. But isn't the latter a greater aspiration? Couldn't it lead to another possibility than the one we are living in now?

One of the reasons I don't demonize all the 70+ million people who elected a man whose behavior I find, frankly, deplorable is because I've spent time with people who think differently than me in what I'd call neutral settings.

For example, my wife and I became RVers during the Covid pandemic. The only way we thought we could see our kids who lived across the country was to drive in our own mini home from Florida to California, stopping only for gas and to sleep. While on the way, we drove through southern United States, places that previously I would have been afraid to drive through.

There were a couple of situations where I felt uncomfortable. Once there was a group of men at the RV campsite who were drinking and rowdy. I didn't think seeing two women together would make them calmer, so we stayed inside. Another time, I called ahead and said we are a female couple, one Black and one white. I asked if we would be safe there. The hesitation on the other end of the line convinced me to change our reservations.

But that was just two out of the seven or eight stops we made. By and large, we were welcomed by people as we pulled in, helped by people as we parked, offered a drink, to sit by a fire, to share stories of the road. Based on where they were from and the way they spoke about our country, we could hear that we had different views. What we had in common was a love of the road, the appreciation of nature, the appreciation of discovery and adventure.

Even if temporarily, we were part of the same tribe and were treated as such. They didn't ask us if we were married, and we didn't always say. We never hid our relationship however, so folks who met us had a chance to see two women together, up close, and it didn't seem to threaten any of them.

We met lovely people from all over the United States, and we enjoyed the journey so much that we made the trip across five times.

Stepping Out of Our Echo Chambers

The way forward includes spending less time in our respective echo chambers.

Like many, I spend too much time on my social media accounts. I think of those spaces as the modern public square. I try to post things that will be a positive contribution to the dialogue. I get a lot of likes on 99 percent of my posts. When I post the rare political thought, I get a lot less. Some of it is because of the algorithm hiding anything controversial, and some of it is folks not wanting to engage.

I notice that when my Jewish-identified friends post about Zionism or about a two-state solution or about Israeli hostages, the most I will do is click on a "care" emoji. I am afraid to say anything they will object to because I don't trust my own point of view. And I don't trust online friendships to withstand disagreements.

I am beginning to make progress on this front.

My ex-husband, the father of my half-Italian son, is right leaning, conservative. He seems to hate anything that smacks of socialism. He thinks socialism made his birth country weak, and he thinks American exceptionalism, capitalism, and personal effort are the true north. We often disagree. He gets to navigate the United States as a wealthy white male, and I don't think that qualifies him to say what it's like for others to be in the U.S.A.

That said, I try to remain open when he posts something about our current (early 2025) situation. He posts his beliefs that those of us who are in love with Zelensky and hate Putin don't understand the history of the region and that NATO over reached, breaking an agreement they made with Russia. In his view, Russia's invasion of Ukraine is in retaliation.

But instead of "yelling" in cyberspace, I stopped and went to do some research. I am learning more about the region and the history. Although I don't agree with him on what the best or right outcome is for Ukraine, I understand better why he thinks the way he does.

What does this understanding benefit? We stay in open communication. I learned something, and he has a chance to learn from me because I did not dismiss him. I intend to check in with him about a few of the most disturbing acts coming from the White House. How he answers will let me know where he stands. If he has no empathy, our discussions may be over. But if he shows empathy, even while we disagree, there may be an opening.

I realize we can't persuade or even have conversations with everyone. I know that for our own mental health, we need to limit our exposure to ideas that are toxic to us. And yet we can model peaceful demonstrations, boycotts, and peaceful rigorous dialogue that, together, can move us forward. This seems more feasible than staying on our respective sides with our arms folded looking the other way.

Act with Patience and Love

One of the ways for us to move forward is to have patience with some aspects of this process.

Dialogue and understanding take time. Safety is urgent, but social change can be slow. I recall reading about Eleanor Roosevelt and the Universal Declaration of Human Rights. She hosted literal tea parties for months on end and organized discussions for years to help that critical document take form. They took three steps forward and four steps back more than once, but she persevered, believing in what was right and believing that it was possible to get there.

We, too, have big problems to solve. We have climate change that threatens plant life, sea life, wildlife, and human life. We have the hatred and vitriol of racism, sexism, anti-semitism, homophobia, transphobia, and geopolitical conflict. And the list goes on—human trafficking, deforestation, starvation, disease, and war.

We can add to this list and have trouble getting to the end of it, so it's normal to feel overwhelmed. None of these problems has a short-term quick fix. All of them take time to understand and deeper understandings to evaluate options for solutions. Many solutions already exist. If so, then we have the work of persuading the actors to act.

As long as we take steps in the direction of creating the beloved community (which we will examine later in this chapter) and enhancing the love of the Earth, we make progress. Each of us needs to choose which aspect we want to put our attention on. None of us can focus on everything at once, but each of us can chose where to focus. Then we have to have the patience to continue the work, even when it feels frustrating, even if the improvements may not come in our lifetimes.

In addition to patience, we want to move forward acting in love. Remember this scripture: "Love is patient, love is kind. It does not envy, it does not boast, it is not proud. It does not dishonor others, it is not self-seeking, it is not easily angered, it keeps no record of wrongs. Love does not delight in evil but rejoices with the truth. It always protects, always trusts, always hopes, always perseveres. Love never fails."

It's not a coincidence that 1 Corinthians 13: 4-8 is read at most weddings. As the couple embarks on a new life, a new way forward, love is their compass. We will serve ourselves and each other to do the same. If we base all our actions in love, we can find the patience to work for all good things.

Creating the Beloved Community

One of the ways forward is to look for what is good and working.

James and Deborah Fallows's book *Our Towns* demonstrated the hope and possibility that lives throughout the United States. They took a journey of 100,000 miles into the heart of America and found people connecting with one another and creating their versions of beloved community, even though so many of the stories never made the main press. They found that even while national politics are strained, local politics are productive. Neighbors are creating local solutions for problems like drugs, guns, crime, and deterioration. They spent five years meeting people, witnessing their work, and documenting their successes and hope.

If we take the time to look, we can find good happening in our own neighborhoods. Who is helping with the unhoused? Who is helping with the unemployed? Who is helping to beautify? Who is engaging the youth? Who is working to curtail violence and crime? Who is taking care of the elders? And with all that is going on, how can the good be amplified? How can we contribute to it?

- *Continuing the work of creating the beloved community is a way forward*
- *Beloved community doesn't arise without effort.*
- *Beloved community requires care, maintenance, and engagement*

In 1957, Dr. Martin Luther King Jr. first publicly spoke about his vision of the "beloved community." He said, "The aftermath of nonviolence is the creation of beloved community."

When speaking of the beloved community throughout the movement for what can also be called Black Liberation, King emphasized that hate could not be a part of any sustainable future. He said, "I have decided to stick with love. Hate is too great of a burden to bear." While the protests and boycotts and sit-ins were designed to change laws and behavior, the true endgame was a community that supported every person in it, enabling each to reach their highest potential.

King wanted all people to have the freedom to sit, vote, live, and flourish wherever they chose, rather than leaving some shut out. We do well to remember it was just roughly sixty years ago that people categorized as Black were given the right to vote in elections, sit at a lunch counter, sit anywhere on the bus and expect to be protected under the same laws as everyone else.

King and a predominant swath of the Civil Rights leaders in the 1960s ascribed to nonviolence. They were educated in its tenets, committed to it, and executed it without pause for a decade until his murder in 1968.

Some folks like to say, "That's the past. Let's stop bringing it up." I say, "We have to understand from where we have come to understand where we are now." The attitudes, beliefs, and behaviors that excluded Black people from everyday freedoms did not disappear when the laws changed.

Remember how Ruby Bridges had to be escorted to school by the National Guard in 1960? That resistance to her presence brought out a throng of people. The hatred and vitriol spewed at her did not dissipate. It went underground and within the people who nurtured and harbored it. Some of those people passed on their hate to the next generation.

We have so much work to do to—and that is the way forward, the Civil Rights, the liberation of all people, the creation and nurturance of the beloved community is a long-term effort.

So many organizations and people today continue the work that Dr. King, John Lewis, Ruby Bridges, Rosa Parks, and others risked and even gave their lives to affect. The prospect of communities based on mutual love and respect are not a pipe dream but a very real opportunity. And while I used an example of what affected Black people, the creation of beloved community affects *all* people. When we are all free to pursue our best lives, we all benefit. Living in a context of peace and opportunity for all is a better life for everyone. And it is hard to get to, but it's worth working toward every day.

I got distracted by consumerism and comfort and stopped working diligently toward creating the beloved community. It's time to take up the charge again.Some of it will look the same: protests, legislative pressure, boycotts, campaigns, marches. Some of our actions may need to be different, starting with our personal attitudes and behaviors and including intentional community building, new leadership, a new narrative, and bold actions.

- *Continuing the work of creating the beloved community is a way forward*
- *Beloved community doesn't arise without effort.*
- *Beloved community requires care, maintenance, and engagement*

9

The Way Forward:
Start, Stop, Continue

WITH EVERY WORD I WRITE, I speak to myself, even as I write the word "you." If I become a better community member and citizen by sharing these words, then this was a beneficial effort. If these words inspire a new way forward in you, that is my dream come true.

Let's Start

Start teaching those around you, your children, grandchildren, neighbors, friends. I admire families who take the time to tell ancestral stories, to teach their children what they are not learning in school. There are children in Black families who know more about the history of Black Wall Street than those that live in the neighborhood in Tulsa where a white mob burned it to the ground. These children have the opportunity to form ideas about who they want to be and what they want to do with the context of those who've come before.

My children are half Black and half white. I instilled some Black pride in them, but I could have done more educating. I led by example. I took them with me to school district meetings. They saw me interact with the public. They saw me lead.

What can you consciously teach by your example? What is your family history? What people do you come from? What can telling their stories teach?

When we learn anything about how the world works, anything that might make us kinder to each other, we must teach that, too.

For example, I may have shared the *National Geographic* article on the artificiality of race with one of my children, but I did not share it with all three. And I didn't make time to discuss it with them. I also could have had a salon at my home about the article to engage others in the discussion. Learning together can build community.

Start understanding the system you are in. Start at the very local level. Who are your neighbors? How did this neighborhood develop? What is the history of this place? Of this town? Who are the leaders? What are the values that this community subscribes to? Are those values written down?

From there, we can take the same approach to the region, the state, and the country. Becoming a student again is a posture and an attitude that can bring peace inside and keep you open to learning. Learning about the way decisions are made, learning about who is making them, and learning how you can contribute is part of the way forward.

Start having regular communication with those who represent you. I need to embrace this myself. In a more normal situation, I aspire to write to one representative each month. In the crisis we are experiencing now, I'm committing to writing at least once a week.

The communication can be a thank you, an admonishment, or a request. What if our representatives had regular data to report about their constituents? When I held public office and often met with state-level legislators, I learned how little communication they receive from their constituents. A handful of calls or letters a week was considered a lot, even when most of them represented tens of thousands of constituents. We elect people and then leave them to do their job. However, their job is to represent us. How are they to know what we are passionate about if we do not make demands or share information? Simply reaching out could make a difference to those elected officials who are true servant leaders. And yes, I believe they do exist.

Start being more intentional about your role in your community and in the world. I have thought about this in my own life. I wrote this book to get a greater understanding of my options and to learn how to build on my personal history. Are you clear about who you intend to be? I do not judge what you choose. I only ask, "Are you choosing?"

These are just a few suggestions of things you might start to do. You may already be doing each of them. The theme here is connection. What can you start to do that would contribute to a more beloved community where you are? Are there invitations you can make or places where your presence would make a difference?

I consider myself an introvert because I regain energy and balance by being alone. This sometimes keeps me in my own world for long stretches of time. I can move out of my comfort zone by asking myself to connect with others more often and to offer my presence where it might benefit others, even as it may be inconvenient or something I'd prefer not to do. We can't know exactly how what we think, say, and do affects others, but we can be certain that it does. The ripple effect in our communities is real.

A woman I never met wrote me a note following a conference we both attended. She said throughout the time she was there, she felt invisible and out of place. I walked into a room where she was, and I smiled at her. I smiled at her. That's all. We didn't even exchange words. And she said that act changed the entire experience for her.

We can't know the effect of our presence, but we can know that it has an effect.

Let's Stop

Somethings can be left behind on our way forward.

While there are things we want to start doing, there certainly are also things we want to stop doing. I'm sharing my list here, but you'll have your own.

Stop enriching billionaires as much as possible. For me, this means not using Amazon as my private shopping mall anymore. I got so addicted to point-and-click living that my neighbor politely said, "Wow! You two get boxes every day." It was true.

I noticed that I was buying things that came from all over the world—and more and more from China. I wasn't thinking about the implications of my choices, about who was affected and how.

I once read a powerful piece called "The Story of Stuff" that explained who and what is exploited so that you and I could pay so little for something. The young woman who wrote the graphic tale started by being curious about a $5 radio she considered buying. How could it cost so little? Her inquiry led her to learn about how much deforestation, unfair labor practices, and climate disruption were part of her inexpensive product.

Learning all of this slowed down my buying and enhanced my consciousness about what I bought for a while. I don't remember consciously ignoring what I learned, but I conveniently forgot about it as I made order after order, "saving money." As I write this, I've been Amazon sober for more than six months. It seems like no big deal, but it's life changing. I get up and walk or drive to a store to buy the thing there. I look up the company and order direct from their website and wait longer for it to arrive. And I rethink whether or not I really need the thing.

Use your spending as a form of communication with society. In addition to Amazon, are there other companies or brands whose business practices are counter to your values? Be inconvenienced and don't contribute to their profits. As the current administration removes more and more regulations on businesses, we must speak with our resources about the society we want to see. This means doing research. For example, I do not want to contribute to the private prison industry. Who owns that? I don't want to contribute to the food industry giants that put too much sugar and toxins in our food for their profit. What brands do I want to avoid? What brands do I want to promote?

The billionaire class appears to want to return to the "Gilded Age." This would threaten labor laws, safety regulations, food safety, pharmaceutical regulation, environmental protections, and so much more. What do you want instead? If we don't have an alternative vision, we may find ourselves living in theirs.

Stop obsessing about having a perfect body. For myself, I want to stop the body image obsession. By that, I don't mean I want to stop paying attention to my health. What I do mean is obsessing how much fat my body stores, what's lumpy, what's loose, what's wrinkling. I have spent thousands of dollars and countless days—years even—on one protocol or another only to eventually return to a curvy body padded with fat. Time to move on and dedicate that energy to contributing to others, instead of perfecting myself.

Some people who know me consider me a "self-help" guru. In that light, I will not abandon self-care, tenderness, or love of self. What I want is to stop spending an inordinate amount of energy resisting what is. My body perfectly reflects my life as I am living it —how much food I enjoy, what type; how much exercise I do, how often; how much stress I experience, how often; how much anxiety and worry I process, how often; how much sleep I get, how often. All of these things and decisions create the body that carries me. I accept and do my best each day and appreciate this body, as I wrote in a poem I called "This Old Tree": Every lump, knot, wrinkle, and sag are evidence I have lived. What would serve you to stop resisting or obsessing on?

Stop staying on the surface of things. Being overly concerned about my physical appearance is one of the ways I have lived superficially. I want to stop doing that. I want to accept life as it comes and engage with it as it comes. I need to contemplate what it looks like to engage with life more deeply.

For example, I have added my pronouns under my name on Zoom. Have I actually considered why I answer to she/her?

I also have noticed at the start of meetings that some people acknowledge the land "un-ceded" by a particular Indigenous group. I have heard an Indigenous elder admonish that this is superficial unless we connect in other ways with the fight for recognition, reconciliation, and justice.

Is it enough to wear a "Black Lives Matter" t-shirt? Is it enough to march and protest? Or do we need to care enough to learn how we contribute to the oppression of others and then change our behavior?

I also have been superficial about knowing my neighbors who have a different view of the world. I have been willing to have amiable exchanges as fellow RVers, but do I want to sit at a table and have a talk? I don't know what exactly I will do, but I do know I am now interested in using my skills to specifically heal this divide right where I am.

In some ways I have prepared for this moment, as have you. What skills do you have that can contribute to creating a beloved community? You don't have to be a leader, but you could stop avoiding any event or conversation that makes you uncomfortable. You could stop saying, "I don't do politics," and see what that makes possible.

Stop being hypocritical. If I care about the environment and continue to drive and fly as often as I do, can I claim to care? Or is it more honest to start with, "I'm concerned about the environment, but I'm not willing to drive less and travel less." "I'm concerned about homelessness, but I'm not willing to give up either of my homes, one in the U.S. and the other in Italy." "I'm concerned about human trafficking, but I'm mostly concerned about my grandchildren's health and happiness" "I'm concerned about hunger and lack of water, but I'm still going to enjoy an abundant lifestyle."

It is more honest to say, "I will help with problems I see by writing checks and lending a hand when possible, but primarily I am going to enjoy my life." If that is truth for now, recognize that you cannot change what you don't reveal. As I reveal to myself what I actually think, I can decide to think differently.

Stop focusing on Black suffering and focus more on celebrating Black magnificence in my interactions. I need to remember and share that all of humankind began on the African continent. Civilizations such as the Moors, for example, had art, culture, style, and even engineering that outranked the white populations they came into contact with.

When Africans were enslaved and came to the United States in chains and naked, they were still able to influence music, culture, food, and social reforms more than any other population in history. This is also true of us. This is true of your people. We suffered and there still is suffering. But we come from ancestors who were powerful, creative, and magnificent. And all of that runs through us now, just waiting for our recognition. I can stop focusing on our suffering and put my attention and my narrative on what's also true: We are an amazing people.

As you read my list, do you see something in your life that you want to consider stopping? Maybe it's just stopping to look at your life, making sure it's in alignment with what you value. One of the criticisms I've often made of the current administration and the wealthiest among us is that greed is a disease. I have more than I need, so therefore I contribute to a culture of greed. I have to reconcile that with who I want to be in the world. How much is enough? How do I demonstrate enough generosity? In what ways am I behaving exactly the same way as those I say are destroying our social fabric?

Before We Continue

Before we look at those things we want to continue doing toward a more beloved community, I want to say to you and to me: Don't contribute to what you know is wrong. We each have a true north inside of us. We know when something feels right and something feels wrong. Some things are obvious. I know it's wrong to pretend as if Social Security is some form of welfare when it is paid for by people who expect it to be there when they retire. I know it's wrong to spew hatred toward transgender people as if they are responsible for the ills of society. I know it's wrong to make it harder for people to exercise their right to vote. I know it's wrong to seize people and deport them without due process. I know it's wrong to erase the truth of our American history full of genocide, enslavement, and oppression. I know it's wrong for any of us to behave as if we are above the law.

These are things that are clear to me. Others may be more subtle, and I may not always do the right thing. But I can stand up for the truth I know.

We will all make mistakes, and sometimes override our feelings, but we can commit to doing our best to follow our inner guidance every day. I'm writing this from our home in Umbria, Italy. It's a modest home, an apartment, but I know it represents a life most people in the world will not experience. For the first time in more than two decades of coming here for weeks and months at a time, I question whether it is right. Just because I can, do I? Is it right for me to have such a beautiful life when there is so much suffering?

I invite you and me to pay attention. What feels right? What feels wrong? And what will I do now?

I started this chapter with the things we could consider starting, then stopping, but I knew that we would get to the things to continue because we are all doing good where we are. This book is my confession, my wake-up call, and I share it in hopes that you will find it useful as someone looking to be clear about how to live in the new now. I've had a lot to confess, but I also know that I have a lot to share.

At this point you may feel overwhelmed. "I need to start doing some things, stop doing others and continue whatever good I am doing?" I feel you. These ideas are intended to inspire an inner review that only you can do. Only you know what is enough for you to do. Only you know what capacity you have. Only you know if you can add one more thing.

I invite you to consider these things, and at the end of the consideration, you may chose to feel gratitude for the life you have built and are living. And that, too, would be a wonderful outcome for all of us.

Let's Continue

First we disrupt ourselves, we shake off the complacency that naturally occurs, we look at ourselves in the mirror, and we ask, "Am I being the best version of myself today?" And when the answer is no, we gently invite ourselves to allow the next iteration of who we are to emerge. There is no deadline; there is only allowing. If we throw ourselves into action without the peace of choice, our actions are likely to be uncoordinated and out of alignment.

Take a deep breath as you think about the things you will continue to do. Take this list as a celebration, as gratitude for what you have done, and appreciate your own humanity.

Here, then, are my humble suggestions.

Continue doing things that bring you joy. Your joy is an antidote to despair and hopelessness. It is part of the medicine to keep you well so you can contribute to others. Remember the Thích Nhất Hạnh advice that if you let the world's anxiety get into your heart, then you can't help.

Joy is underrated. I have mentored and coached leaders for the past twenty years. When I first started, I'd ask executives, "Where's your joy on your joy meter? From zero to ten?" First, I got a lot of blank stares. Joy? It took many moments to even connect with the concept, and many could not. They did not see how joy fit into their lives, as if joy were an unattainable pipe dream.

Bit by bit, we teased out a few moments in which joy may have creeped in to remind them that it did exist in their experiences. This was necessary for joy to have any chance to grow in their lives. As they nurtured and developed joy, their leadership changed. They became invested in seeing joy experienced by others, creating a more wholistic way of leading. Joy matters to the whole. Your joy matters to the whole. Continue doing things that bring you joy.

Continue to be a force for good. In addition to experiencing and expressing joy, I want to continue in the other ways that I am a force for good. I'll continue to provide support and coaching with a spiritual lens to leaders on the frontlines of social justice. I'll continue to write checks for causes I care about. I'll continue to write things that come through me to inspire and help others.

There are small things I do, and I'll continue those too. I love to color. I bought a pile of canvas bags and fabric pens with the idea to decorate them and fill them with supplies for unhoused people in my community. The bags are a form of art and creativity, and I imbue them with my good wishes with every color and every stroke of the pen. When I deliver them to the center where there are comprehensive services for people without a permanent home, they receive my offering with appreciation and great warmth. The executive director said it is clear that the bags are made with love. This is a small thing, but it connects me with people having a different experience than mine. Now I am inspired to offer to come and talk about one of my books or any subject they think will be helpful. I can get a little closer. As Mother Teresa said, "No act done with great love is small."

Continue to be a force for good where you are. I took inventory of my failures. You should take inventory of your successes. Take inventory of the positive ways you contribute to your community right now. Be generous. Count everything. If you plant flowers in your garden, if you decorate for holidays, if you give away your extra lemons, help a neighbor, check on a neighbor, say hello, convene a neighborhood gathering, volunteer somewhere, you are being a force for good. If you take a walk around the neighborhood and smile, that is also good.

Continue being engaged in your community meetings. Read the local newspaper. Be informed of what affects your neighbors.

I have a near perfect record of voting in all elections. In more than forty-five years of voting, I missed a few statewide elections due to travel and poor planning, but otherwise I made my voice heard. I am even more committed to this now, and wherever I am in the world, I will make sure I do what it takes to stay connected and vote. If you, too, are committed to always voting, maybe help get out the vote in your area. I find this activity to be inspiring. Pre-Covid, I went door to door in neighborhoods, exhorting folks to show up at the polls. Since the pandemic, most of my activism has been by phone or postcard. I will reconsider engaging again in person for 2028.

Continue being loving and kind in every circle you join. Whether in line at the grocery or pharmacy, or at a local town hall meeting, or just joining a neighbor on a walk, offer your presence with a smile or a greeting. Take time to meet someone in your neighborhood you don't know. Be willing to tell them why you are doing it. Let them know you want to contribute to a more beloved community, one where we all feel safe, cared for, and where we can thrive.

Continue to trust that we live in a friendly universe. Trust most people are good, that they want to be loved and to love. I want to continue not being afraid of someone who is different from me. I want to have boundaries that are healthy but not walls that can't be traversed.

This fundamental belief about how the world works, how we are all connected, how each of us matters to the whole needs to continue to be the underpinning of all that I say and do. What do you want to continue believing about humans, life, connections, and what do you trust?

Embrace Your True North

Here is my summary list. What is yours?

- **Start** teaching those around you,
- **Start** understanding the system you are in.
- **Start** having regular communication with those who represent you.
- **Start** being more intentional.

- **Stop** enriching billionaires.
- **Stop** obsessing about having a perfect body.
- **Stop** staying on the surface of things.

- **Stop** being hypocritical.
- **Stop** focusing on Black suffering (or any other).

- **Continue** doing things that bring you joy.
- **Continue** to be a force for good.
- **Continue** being engaged.
- **Continue** being loving and kind.
- **Continue** to trust that we live in a friendly universe.

We have and feel our true north. We know when we rationalize destructive behavior, whether with our own bodies, the Earth's body, or the collective community body. We know.

10

Claim Our Abundance

WHEN I BEGAN this conversation with you, I spoke about how I didn't act in situations of injustice because I didn't learn enough or care enough to take the best action. All of our actions derive from how we think. And our thinking is informed by what we study and learn. For more than a decade, I have been learning about claiming prosperity and abundance so that it doesn't seem as if only certain people have access to them.

Recently, I listened to journalist and commentator Joy Reid describe the history of taxation and the desires of some extremely wealthy people to maintain the income gap and suppress any social safety net or anti-poverty programs. As I listened, I considered how to respond to that. While I oppose destroying the social safety nets and promoting poverty, I don't oppose wealth in and of itself. Rather than making the wealthy wrong for being rich, why not have a mindset that is open to the possibility of greater wealth, prosperity, and abundance for everyone?

We already examined the nature of greed, but consider that perhaps greed and wealth don't have to be synonymous. Wealth can be enjoyed and used for the greater good based on how you earn it and how you share it.

This is not to ignore the broader economy and its affects on peoples lives: availability of jobs, ongoing discrimination, low wages, high costs, and other factors. Our discussion here is about using our minds to focus on other possible futures: a future in which each person believes they can improve their circumstances first by changing their mind about what is possible.

In his 1937 book *Think and Grow Rich,* writer Napoleon Hill talks about things we can control, such as our desire, our faith, our imagination, and even our intuition. The important thing about this book, and all the books written on the subject of abundance, is to be open to the possibility that wealth is not out of reach for you. There are degrees of wealth, and you may not achieve millionaire or billionaire status, but you may move from where you are today to a future of abundance. And you can help lift up others in compassion, using your abundant resources.

There have also been books written about what is called our "money blueprint." We all inherited ideas about money and wealth from our parents and other adults. It's worth looking at what your blueprint is and how it is or is not serving you today. I find that people who care only about wealth spend all their time accumulating it and managing it and growing it. I find many people who care about doing good treat wealth as a negative or a neutral aspect of their lives.

How might the world be if more people who wanted a better world for everyone allowed themselves the wealth to make a greater difference?

What I Believe

I bring this idea up, knowing it is controversial and may upset or anger some readers. In the spirit of transparency, I must speak about what I believe, even if my beliefs are ridiculed or dismissed.

If I believe the universe to be an abundant source of good for every person in it, I must extend to you the invitation to see for yourself.

I have colleagues and friends who live in many different circumstances all over the world. Whether they are walking ten miles to the nearest available internet station or navigating martial law or war, their individual mentalities about their agency to prosper and live more abundantly are still relevant.

When you are worried every day about your safety, you may

not have any capacity to think about anything else. In that case, those of us who have the freedom to focus on abundance and prosperity have all the more reason to do so.

If you have the capacity, look into your own heart and mind and find ways you can be open to more and more abundance in your life. If you are in circumstances that don't allow you to focus there right now, know that others are doing so on your behalf.

We are made of the same stuff. We share a planet. And what each of us thinks, says and does matters to the whole.

Shift Our Focus to APPLY

Therefore, in addition to voting, protesting, marching, boycotting, and being in community, what if we focus also on what I call "APPLY"— abundance, prosperity, peace, love, and yes!

Let's break this down:

Abundance is the truth of life. Life is abundant. Abundance is not about money or things. Instead, it's about noticing, being aware, taking in all life offers. Abundance in nature is an example for all of us. Just look at the different types of plants, leaves, trees that surround you, even if you are in a city. Look at the different birds, bugs, animals. Look at the clouds in the sky. Without being able to name them, you can still see the abundance. There is an abundance of air we all breathe. We take for granted the abundance of available water in the United States. While water is abundant on Earth, it is not universally shared or available.

Prosperity is the outcome of an abundance mindset, a mindset in which you notice, focus on, and are grateful for all that surrounds you. With this mindset, you draw more good into your life. Receptivity, coupled with awareness, is the key. Go back to the fundamentals. Look at your beliefs about wealth. Do you confuse the often cited, "Money is the root of all evil," with the actual scripture, "The *love of money* is the root of all evil." More people who intend to do good, to share, and to support others having wealth is good for the whole. Sometimes we get stuck in the binary, such as thinking we can be rich or we can be good social activists. In fact, we can be rich social activists if we are mindful about our priorities and how we build wealth. My wise niece reminds me that feeling bad about my good is counterproductive. If you grew up poor, you might feel guilty about having a measure of wealth. Please don't.

The founder and owner of Patagonia offers an example of a wealthy social activist, as he turned his flourishing company over to a nonprofit that works for the future health of this planet. Instead of enriching shareholders, he chose to invest in future generations. There are ways to be that we haven't discovered or considered yet. Having a prosperity mindset keeps us open to the possibilities.

Peace within is a tremendous contribution we can make to creating the beloved community. Finding our own inner peace is a gift to everyone we encounter, and it invites others to find theirs. Having more of us searching for and finding peace within makes for more peaceful relationships, families, communities, and nations. Peace within as a movement can change the world, one heart and mind at a time. This is something over which each of us has control. No one can control our inner landscape, where we have absolute dominion. Choosing peace is a powerful position of leadership that begins on the inside.

Love, always love, as the center point, the well from which we draw our energy. Love is the fuel for life, the true north. Imagine love-infused prosperity, and you can imagine a new world. What is your relationship with love today? Is it romantic love that you feel for your partner? Do you have love for nature, remembering that we as humans are a part of nature? On what basis do you make decisions? Is it logic or is there heart involved? Staying in the inquiry of what love looks like reminds me of a quote from philosopher Dr. Cornell West: "Justice is what love looks like in public." In what ways does moving with and from love contribute to justice?

Yes! Say yes to abundance, prosperity, peace, and love. Say yes to a greater and greater expression of who you are in the world. Say yes to your authentic self, yes to your own awareness of abundance, yes to your personal prosperity. What we say yes to finds its way to us. Yes is a powerful word. Living in a yes mentality is more energizing than living in a no mentality, and yes moves us forward, being *for* things rather than pushing against things. What do you say yes to? Can you lead with your yes rather than spending most of your effort defending against your no? Where does it makes sense for you to focus on the yes? Here are some things I say yes to: I am for safety and freedom for transgender people. I am for accurate accounts of history. I am for including all views at the table to get to agreement. I say yes to collaboration and cooperation. I say yes to the rule of law.

To APPLY ourselves is to offer a direct response to the systems of wealth and power that try to keep the rest of us down. We counteract the intention to remove all safety nets by having resources ourselves and sharing them with others. We don't give up on changing laws or voting in responsible and sane representatives. We position ourselves to have more influence and more capacity to act.

This is another opportunity to withdraw from the tyranny of the *OR*. We can be wealthy *or* we can be good. We can be abundant, prosperous, peaceful, loving *and* aligned with YES to all of it.

The way forward begins with a mindset of abundance, prosperity, peace, love, and yes.

Where some folks and systems are about hoarding wealth, about greed, about keeping people poor, we can respond by being about abundance prosperity, peace, love, yes!

APPLY: Abundance, Prosperity, Peace, Love, Yes!

11

Redemption

I TITLED THIS CHAPTER "REDEMPTION," the act of saving something, making up for something. Redemption includes forgiveness, salvation, emancipation, deliverance. I seek for a new way of engaging with life to redeem the parts of me that were not available to pay attention, to learn, grow, and act. I trust I have within me all that is needed to find a new way.

Redemption often is associated with religious concepts. To be forgiven of sins, for example, is redemption. I have learned that the definition of sin, as the word was used in many biblical stories, translates to "missing the mark." I'm OK with this idea. In my life, I often have missed the mark. Redemption reminds me to make the effort again and trust that, with practice, I will get better at hitting the mark. I do need to know what I am aiming for, which brings me full circle. To be the best version of myself, I need to respect and love who I am and move as someone who is respected and loved. I want to continue to live with an open heart as much as possible and give everyone I encounter the chance to experience love as me.

As I write this, three men are moving around our Italian apartment, trying to solve a chimney problem in the apartment below us. They have on dirty boots, are traipsing in and out of the house, leaving doors wide open, climbing on the roof, going into the attic, yelling to each other. This has been going on for three hours now. We turned off our heat because it was being wasted.

In this situation, how can I show up as my best self? I used my poor Italian to ask what was happening. They gave me the answer:

They are trying to solve the problem, but they are not done. I smiled and said thank you, even though my floor is dirty, I don't have silence to write, and we have family arriving tomorrow.

I step back and look out the window at the river and remember why I love it here. I look over at the pasta we are about to cook and the sauce bubbling on the stove. And I know: I can be love in action right now.

Every day, I pay attention to how I am being and acting, asking what I need to know. It's uncomfortable, and I'm losing some sleep, but it's necessary. The world is constantly changing, always has been, and always will. The question for me is whether I will continue to grow and change with it. Will I be part of the evolution of humankind?

I still experience the dark, and I won't give myself a pass out of it until I decide who I'm going to be when I emerge. Writing this book is just the beginning of a new understanding. I have taken inventory of who I have been. I have taken inventory of what I have done for the common good. I have taken inventory of what I have not done that contributed to a divided country, consolidated power, and hopelessness for too many.

In the dark place of my guilt, sadness, and fear about what is next, I find it perfect that I'm complaining about people disrupting my quiet in my second home. This is not a problem. A problem is people losing Social Security and Medicare and jobs and safety and hope.

Maybe if I get some perspective on this, I'll be a more useful person. Maybe I'll be someone who is more interested in the quality of life for all people over the quality of my next meal, vacation, or other privileged experience.

At the end of the day, I believe we are all made of the same stuff. We share a planet, and what each of us thinks, says, and does matters to the whole. I believe this, but I have not embodied it. I have let what is unpleasant stay over in a corner, and I decide when I'll take a look. I haven't allowed the full human experience to be part of me, incorporated in how I move on the planet. I'm a little afraid of who I will be when I do, but I am curious now.

I am willing to be open to a new possibility. I am willing to do what makes me come more alive.

Is darkness, after all, more than the absence of light?